BELT UP
thelwell's
MOTORING MANUAL

by Norman Thelwell

ANGELS ON HORSEBACK*
THELWELL COUNTRY*
THELWELL IN ORBIT
A LEG AT EACH CORNER*
A PLACE OF YOUR OWN
TOP DOG*
THELWELL'S RIDING ACADEMY*
UP THE GARDEN PATH*
THE COMPLEAT TANGLER*
THELWELL'S BOOK OF LEISURE*
THE EFFLUENT SOCIETY
PENELOPE*
THREE SHEETS IN THE WIND*
BELT UP*
THIS DESIRABLE PLOT*
THELWELL GOES WEST

*

THELWELL'S HORSE BOX*
(containing *A Leg at Each Corner,
Thelwell's Riding Academy, Angels on
Horseback*, and *Thelwell Country* paperbacks)

*These titles are available in paperback

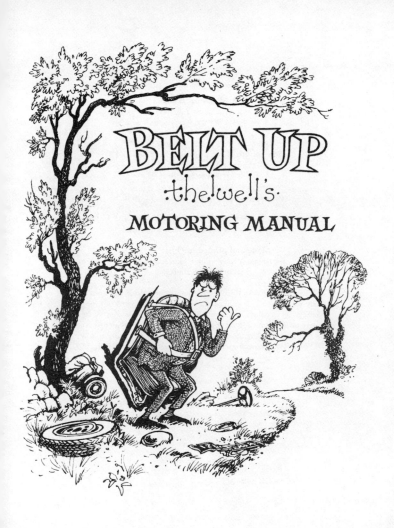

BELT UP

thelwell's

MOTORING MANUAL

MAGNUM BOOKS
Methuen Paperbacks Ltd

A Magnum Book

BELT UP
ISBN 0 417 01090 7

First published 1974 by Eyre Methuen Ltd
Magnum edition published 1977
reprinted 1978

Magnum Books are published by Methuen Paperbacks Ltd
11 New Fetter Lane, London EC4P 4EE

Made and printed in Great Britain
by Richard Clay (The Chaucer Press) Ltd
Bungay, Suffolk

*A number of the situations in this book are based on ideas
which originally appeared in* PUNCH, *and my thanks are due
to the proprietors for permission to use them here.*

Contents

DIAGRAM OF CONTROLS

1. FUEL GAUGE – A steady needle indicates that you have run out of petrol
2. FUEL WARNING LIGHT – To worry you at all times
3. SPEEDOMETER – Needle moves to left automatically on sight of police patrol car
4. CLOCK – Remains stuck at ten minutes to seven
5. BRAKE WARNING LIGHT – Reminds you that brakes may fail at any time
6. GLOVE BOOT – Storage for gloves and boots
7. INDICATOR LEVER – Push up to turn left – down to turn right
8. INDICATOR LEVER WARNING LIGHT – Flashes and ticks loudly when moved
9. INTERNAL LIGHT SWITCH – It is hazardous to use it in the dark
10. HORN BUTTON – To frighten other road users
11. FRESH AIR FAN – Produces an alarming hum
12. IGNITION – (Keys cannot be recovered if doors are slammed. Break glass with jack supplied)
13. IGNITION WARNING LIGHT – Continuous red light indicates an electrical fault (No red light indicates an electrical fault)
14. CAR RADIO – Produces depressing news bulletins and police traffic warnings
15. WINDSCREEN WIPER KNOB – Produces monotonous squeak or throb
16. WINDSCREEN WASHER KNOB – Squirts water jets over roof of vehicle
17. ASH TRAY – Produces twanging noise – Traps fingers – Flies into rear of car
18. BRAKE FLUID RESERVOIR – Do not touch under any circumstances
19. HOT AIR REGULATOR – Produces stupor
20. COLD AIR REGULATOR – Produces neuralgia, ear ache, etc. etc.
21. DEFROSTER VENT – Produces alarming hissing noise
22. GEAR LEVER – Produces ear-splitting screech and/or embarrassment to front seat passengers
23. BRAKE PEDAL – Throws occupants violently forwards
24. CLUTCH PEDAL – Throws occupants violently backwards
25. ACCELERATOR PEDAL – Gives illusions of power
26. HAND BRAKE – Produces a smell of burning and poor engine performance
27. HAND BRAKE RELEASE BUTTON – Produces sore thumb
28. BONNET LOCK RELEASE – Releases bonnet lock except at the garage
29. REAR VIEW MIRROR – Produces comical lop-sided view of back seat passengers
30. SAFETY BELTS – Produces mind-bending debates and arguments

TECHNICAL TERMS

A RICH MIXTURE

SAFETY BELT

REV COUNTER

GOOD ROAD CLEARANCE

CRANK SHAFT

DISTRIBUTOR

GEAR SHIFT

AIR INTAKE

VARIABLE JET

OPTIONAL EXTRAS

A RACING CHANGE

BAFFLE PLATE

LEVEL CROSSING

COOLING SYSTEM

STATIC ELECTRICITY

ROTOR ARM

CARBON BRUSH

WIPERS

SILENCER

TORQUE

CHOKE

BIG END

MEN AND THEIR MOTORS

" HELLO! YOUR MOTHER'S OUT OF BED AGAIN "

" ROLL ON THE DAY WHEN CARS GO FASTER THAN SOUND. "

" THERE'S NO USE IN CRYING OVER IT , CHARLIE "

" I'VE LOCATED THE TROUBLE

— LOOSE CHANGE ON THE BEDSIDE TABLE "

" THE ENGINE'S RUNNING DEAD QUIET,

SHE WON'T BACK-FIRE AND I CAN'T GET THE RADIATOR TO BOIL "

" YOU MEAN THEY GAVE YOU A HOME IMPROVEMENT GRANT ? "

" I'VE GOT A THREE LITRE ROVER AT THE MOMENT
        - ABOUT A MILE OUTSIDE SALFORD. "

" YOUR LICENCE HAS RUN OUT "

WOMEN AT THE WHEEL

"DON'T PANIC, CYNTHIA, IT'S GRAVY!"

" DOES THE GAS-STOVE AFFECT THE NO-CLAIMS BONUS? "

" I'LL BE ALRIGHT AFTER A LIE DOWN "

" I LEFT MY PURSE IN THE GLOVE COMPARTMENT "

" IT'S THE FIRST TIME WE'VE USED THE SUN-SHINE ROOF "

" MY SAFETY-BELT'S STUCK "

" A YELLOW PLASTIC BOX MARKED 'SUGAR' "

" THE CAN OPENER'S JAMMED "

" I'LL TRY A NUMBER FOUR IRON "

" LOOK AT THE DEPTH OF THAT CARPET "

" HANG ON , WE'VE BEEN HERE BEFORE "

" SHE JUST KEEPS ON ASKING

WHETHER HER INSURANCE COMPANY'S SOLVENT. "

" ARE WE ON BBC OR ITV ? "

" HELP ME GET HIM INTO BED   I'LL DO THE DRIVING. "

CHILDREN'S CORNER

" HE JUST SAID HIS FIRST WORD — IDIOT "

" THEY'RE LOVELY KIDS — ALWAYS GIVING ME SOMETHING "

" TURN ROUND AND HEAD FOR THE AMUSEMENT ARCADE "

HOW TO HAVE AN ACCIDENT

ON NO ACCOUNT LEAVE THE SCENE OF THE INCIDENT

TAKE THE NUMBER OF ANY OTHER VEHICLE INVOLVED

AND THE NAME AND ADDRESS OF ANY EYE WITNESS

IF YOU HAVE A CAMERA TAKE PHOTOGRAPHS

MAKE NO APOLOGIES OR ADMISSIONS OF GUILT

IF PERSONAL INJURY IS INVOLVED -

IT MAY BE ADVISABLE TO CALL THE POLICE

IF NOT - SIMPLY EXCHANGE NAMES AND ADDRESSES

HAVE A MEDICAL CHECK-UP AS SOON AS POSSIBLE

YOU HAVE BEEN WARNED

YOUR RADIATOR IS BOILING

CAUTION! UMBRELLA FACTORY ON LEFT

DUMPING OF CARS PROHIBITED

BEWARE OF TYRE SLASHERS

YOU ARE SITTING TOO LOW BEHIND THE WHEEL

FREE BRA WITH EVERY FOUR GALLONS

FAMILY PLANNING CLINIC AHEAD

THE DRIVER IN FRONT IS DRUNK

RAILWAY MUSEUM AHEAD

YOU ARE ABOUT TO BE STRUCK BY A THUNDERBOLT

BEWARE OF NAILS ON THE ROAD

SELF SERVICE ONLY

BEWARE OF LOW FLYING MOTOR CYCLES

DRAUGHT BEER AT NEXT PUB

YOUR LEFT EYE IS STRONGER THAN YOUR RIGHT

HOW TO GIVE A DRIVING LESSON

" OK ! SWITCH ON "

" YOU'RE IN GEAR "

" NOW GENTLY INTO FIRST "

" **DEPRESS THE CLUTCH
DEPRESS THE CLUTCH**

"LET THE CLUTCH OUT –
YOU'RE SLOWING"

"GENTLY! GENTLY!"

"NOW CHANGE UP"

"NOT WITH BOTH HANDS!"

" STOP THE CAR "   " **STOP THE CA-A-A-A-R** "

" HOW WAS THAT ? "

" EXCELLENT! YOU'LL MAKE A VERY FINE INSTRUCTOR.

DO'S AND DONT'S FOR DRIVERS

DO MAKE SURE THAT YOUR VEHICLE IS ROADWORTHY
BEFORE STARTING OUT ON A JOURNEY —

DO STOP AND STRETCH YOUR LEGS FROM TIME TO TIME —

OR HAVE A SHORT REST IN SOME SUITABLE SPOT

DO KEEP WELL AWAY FROM DRUGS –

86

— ALCOHOL AND EXCESSIVE SPEED

DO CHECK ALL KNOCKING NOISES IMMEDIATELY —
IT MAY SAVE YOU A GREAT DEAL OF TROUBLE LATER

AND LEARN ENOUGH ABOUT YOUR VEHICLE
TO CARRY OUT MINOR REPAIRS

DO OBEY ALL ROAD SIGNS EXACTLY —

AND DO TAKE EXTRA CARE WHEN APPROACHING SCHOOLS—
CHILDREN ARE NOT ALWAYS THINKING ABOUT TRAFFIC

IF IN REAL TROUBLE DO ASK FOR ASSISTANCE — BUT

DO **NOT** NEGLECT YOUR TYRES –

THE POLICE MAY INSPECT THEM AT ANY TIME

DO NOT RETALIATE
    WHEN OTHER DRIVERS ARE BAD MANNERED –

—OR ALLOW SMALL IRRITATIONS
TO CHANGE YOUR PERSONALITY

DO NOT REVERSE YOUR VEHICLE WITHOUT MAKING SURE
THAT THERE IS NOTHING BEHIND YOU —

OR ACCELERATE WHEN OTHERS ARE TRYING TO OVERTAKE

DO NOT BE TOO AMBITIOUS
WHEN TOWING THINGS ON THE HIGHWAY

OR DRIVE AN EXCESSIVELY NOISY VEHICLE

DO NOT DRIVE OVER FARMLAND
WITHOUT OBTAINING PERMISSION

OR PARK IN UNAUTHORIZED PLACES —

AND ABOVE ALL —

DO NOT GET FLUSTERED IN HEAVY TRAFFIC

DRIVERS FRANTIC

DOMESTIC

MANIC

CAUSTIC

ROMANTIC

OPTIMISTIC

PATHETIC

APOLOGETIC

ANGELIC

ACADEMIC

ECCLESIASTIC

SYMBOLIC

CLAUSTROPHOBIC

EMBRYONIC

CATASTROPHIC

PESSIMISTIC

ERRATIC

ENTHUSIASTIC

BUCOLIC

APATHETIC

SYMPATHETIC

COMIC

PSYCHEDELIC

DOGMATIC

IRONIC

GIGANTIC

PARALYTIC

How to Get Rid of Your Car

TRY TO SELL IT PRIVATELY —

FIND OUT WHAT THE TRADE WILL OFFER —

OR WHAT A BREAKERS YARD CAN DO FOR YOU

YOU MAY DECIDE TO ABANDON IT IN A TRAFFIC JAM —

OR SOME OTHER SUITABLE PLACE

RESULTS MAY BE OBTAINED BY NEGLECTING THE HANDBRAKE

WHILE THE MORE ADVENTUROUS MAY PREFER TO TRY A SWITCH

— BUT IF YOU ARE REALLY DESPERATE ——

PARK IT NEAR AN ADVENTURE PLAYGROUND